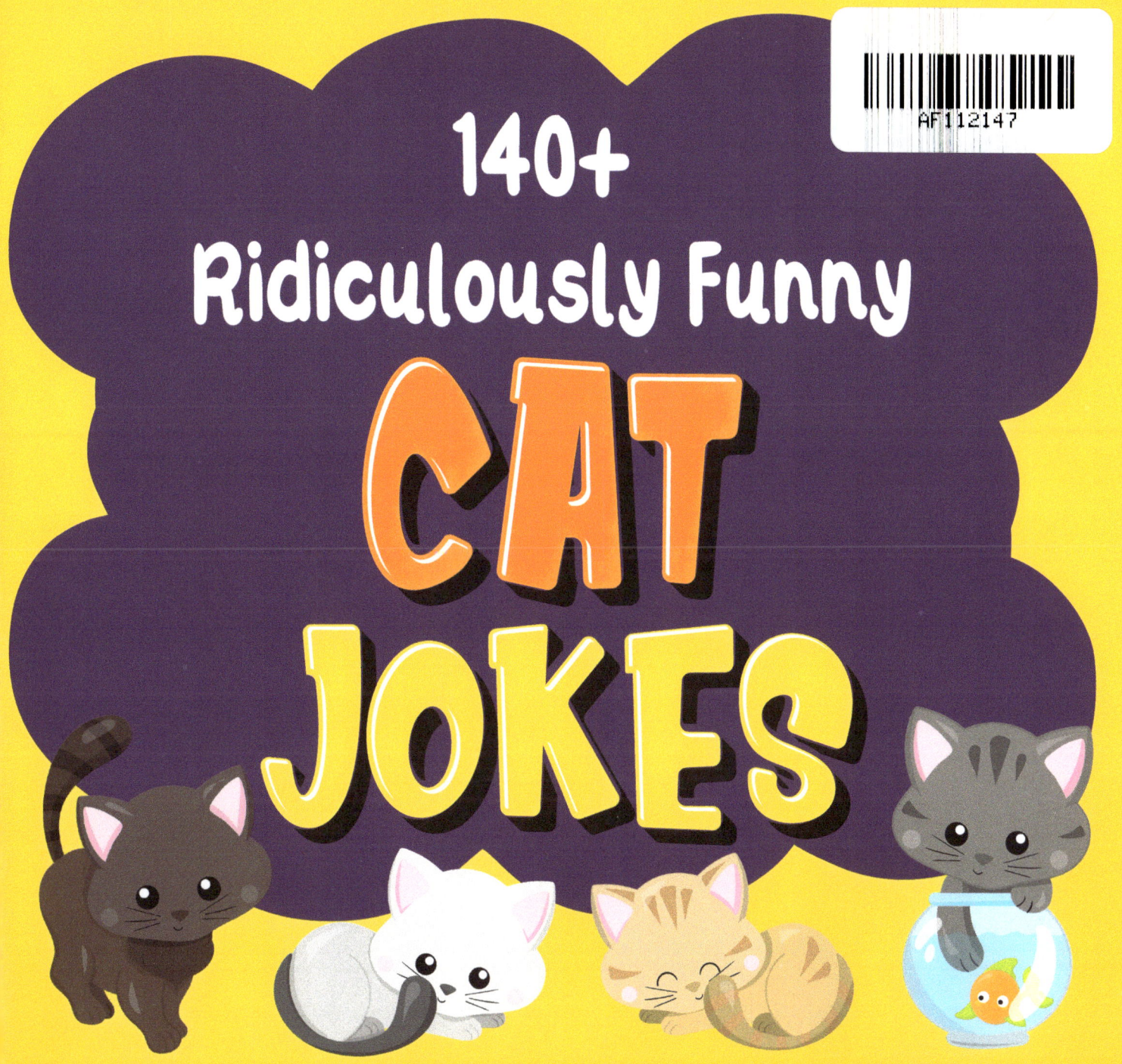

Q: How do cats get over a fight?
A: They hiss and make up!

Q: What do you call a cat that gets anything it wants?
A: Purrr-suasive!

A man takes his cat to the vet because he is cross-eyed. The vet says, "Let's have a look," and picks up the cat to examine his eyes. After looking at his eyes for a while, the vet says, "I'm going to have to put him down." "Wait, what?" the man replies, "Just because he is cross-eyed? "Vet: "No, because he is really heavy!"

Q: What do you call a painting of a cat?
A: A paw-trait!

A cat walks into a job center. "Wow, a talking cat," says the clerk. "With your talent, I'm sure we can find you a gig in the circus." "The circus?", says the cat, disappointed, "What does a circus want with a carpenter?"

Q: Why was the cat disqualified from the poker game?
A: It was a cheetah!

Q: What is a cat's favorite movie?
A: The Sound of Meowsic!

Two cats are sitting in front of bird's cage and observe a newly arrived green canary. One cat says to the other, "It really is a strange color for a bird. Maybe he's not ripe yet."

Q: Why was the cat such a good storyteller?
A: He knew how to paws for dramatic effect!

Q: Why do cats make terrible dance partners?
A: They've got two left feet!

Q: What is the first thing a cat does in the morning? A: It wakes up. Q: What is the second thing it does after waking up? A: It goes back to sleep...

Three cats were sitting together on the rug. The first cat said, "Meow." The second cat also said, "Meow." Then, the third cat said, "Meow, meow." The first cat said, "Hey, don't change the subject!"

Did you hear about the cat who swallowed a ball of wool? She had mittens!

Q: What did the cat say when he lost all his money?
A: I'm paw!

Q: What is the cat's favorite TV show?
A: The evening mews!

While mending fences out on the range, a very religious cowboy lost his favorite Bible. He was devastated! Three weeks later, however, a cat walked up to him, carrying that same Bible in its mouth. The cowboy was astonished, he couldn't believe it! He took the precious book out of the cat's mouth, thanked him, went on his knees and exclaimed: "It's a miracle!". To which the cat replied: "Not really. Your name is written inside the cover."

Q: Why was the cat scared of the tree?
    A: Because of its bark!

Q: What do you call a flying cat?
A: I'm-paws-sible!

Q: How many cats can you put into an empty box?
A: Only one. After that, the box isn't empty!

Q: What do you get if you cross a dog and a cheetah?
A: A dog that chases cars – and catches them!

Q: What do you call a pile of kittens?
A: A meowntain!

A woman sits in a restaurant. All of a sudden, a cat walks in, buys a banana ice cream and leaves. The woman is astounded: "Wow, that's so strange!". The restaurant manager: "Yeah, I agree, up until today she always ordered strawberry ice cream!"

Knock, knock.
Who's there?
Kitten.
Kitten, who?
Quit kitten around and open the door!

Q: What award do cat journalists earn?
A: The Purr-litzer prize!

Q: What do you call a confused cat?
A: Purr-plexed!

Q: How do you make a cat happy?
A: Send it to the Canary Islands!

Q: How does a lion greet the other animals in the field?
A: "Pleased to eat you!"

A mother mouse and a baby mouse are walking along when suddenly a cat attacks them. The mother mouse shouts "WOOF!" and the cat runs away, scared. "See?" the mother mouse says to her baby. "Now do you see why it's important to learn a foreign language?"

Q: What is a cat's favorite car?
A: Catillac!

Q: What do you call a cat that gives up?
A: a quitty!

Q: What do you get if you cross a cat with a dark horse?
A: Kitty Perry!

Q: What do you get if you cross a tiger with a snowman?
A: Frostbite!

Q: Why was the cat so small?
A: When it grew up, it only ate condensed milk!

Did you hear about the cat who invented the knock knock joke? She won the no-bell prize!

Did you hear about the cat who joined the Red Cross? She became a first aid kit!

Knock, Knock!
Who's there?
Claw.
Claw who?
It's Claw Enforcement. You have the right to remain silent. Anything you say or do may be used against you in a court of meow.

Q: How does a cat sing scales?
A: Do-re-mi-ow!

A young girl felt bad after she accidentally let the neighbor's cat get loose. After 2 weeks, the missing cat seemed to be gone for good. "I'm so sorry," the girl told the neighbor. "I'd like to replace it for you." "O.K.," the neighbor said. "How good are you at catching mice?"

Q: What kind of sports car does a cat drive?
A: A Furrari!

Q: What happened when the lion ate the comedian?
A: He felt funny!

Q: What's more amazing than a talking cat?
A: A spelling bee!

One day, a man visited his friend. When he walked into the living room, he found his friend playing chess with his cat. Astonished, he watched the game for a couple of minutes. "I can't believe my eyes!" he exclaimed. "That is the smartest cat I have ever seen." To which his friend replied: "Mwoah, he's not that smart. I've beaten him three games out of five."

Q: Why did the cat wear a dress?
A: She was feline fine!

Did you hear about the cat that climbed the Himalayas? She was a sher-paw!

A man took his guinea pig to the vet. The doctor shook his head as he looked at the guinea pig. "I'm sorry, I'm afraid your guinea pig is dead" said the vet. "Wait, what, how could you be so sure?" the man replied.

So the vet left the room and come back with a Labrador Retriever. The dog stood up on its hind legs, sniffed the guinea pig and shook its head. Next, the vet left the room again. This time, he came back with a cat. The cat also sniffed the guinea pig and also shook its head. The vet said that the guinea pig was 100% dead.

With the man still in shock, the vet handed him the bill.

He looked at the bill, in disbelief: "$500, why $500?" The vet replied "If you had believed me when I first said it, it would have been $75. But you didn't believe me. So, to confirm the death, you also had a lab report and a cat scan!"

Q: Why did the cat put the letter "M" into the fridge?
A: Because it turns "ice" into "mice"!

Knock, Knock!
Who's there?
Neil!
Neil who?
Neil down and pet the cat before he loses his temper!

Q: What do cats wear to smell good?
A: Purr-fume!

Q: Which state has the most cats?
A: Petsylvania!

Q: What do you use to comb a cat?
A: A catacomb!

Q: Why can't cats work the TV remote when watching Netflix?
A: Because they always hit the 'paws' button!

Q: What kind of musician do cats like to be?
A: Purr-cussionists!

Two moms discuss how to get their sons to wake up in the morning, to get them to school on time. "How do you get your sleepy-head son up in the morning?", the first mom asked. The other mom replied, "I just put the cat on the bed." "Huh, how does that help?" The other mom: "The dog's already there..."

Q: Why is it so hard for leopards to hide?
A: Because they're always spotted!

Q: What is the name of the film about a killer lion that swam underwater?
A: 'Claws!'

Q: In what month do cats meow the least?
A: February, it's the shortest month!

A cat sits in a bar, sipping a whiskey. A customer walks up to him and says, "Wow, it's not often that I see a cat drinking whiskey here!" To which the cat replies: "Yeah, but that's hardly a surprise at these prices."

Q: Who did cats vote for in the 2016 United States presidential election?
    A: Hillary Kitten!

    Q: What's a cat's favorite dessert?
A: mice cream!

A cat went to the post office to send a telegram. He took out a blank form and wrote: "Meow. Meow. Meow. Meow. Meow. Meow. Meow. Meow. Meow." When he was done, he gave it to the clerk. The clerk looked at the paper and said to the cat: "There are only 9 words here. We have a special offer: You could send another 'Meow' for the same price." To which the cat replied: "Sorry, but that wouldn't make any sense at all!"

Q: Why don't cats like online shopping?
A: They prefer a cat-alogue!

Q: What happens when it rains cats and dogs?
A: You can step in a poodle!

Q: What do you call at cat that goes bowling?
A: An alley cat!

Q: What is a cat's favorite chocolate bar?
A: Kit Kat!

Q: Who delivers presents to cats on Christmas Eve?
A: Santa Claws!

Q: What do you get when you cross a cat with a parrot?
A: A carrot!

Q: Why was the cat so crabby?
A: He was in a bad mewd!

Q: What do you call a cat in a station wagon?
A: A car-pet!

Q: Where is one place that your cat can sit, but you can't?
A: Your lap!

Q: What happened when the cat went to the flea circus?
A: She stole the show!

Q: Is it bad luck if a black cat follows you?
A: That depends on whether you're a human or a mouse!

Q: What do you call a cat race?
A: A meowathon!

Q: How do you call someone who's addicted to cats?
A: A catholic!

Q: How is cat food sold?
A: Usually purr can!

Q: What do you call an obese cat?
A: Meow-sive!

Q: How does a cat get what it wants?
A: With friendly purrsuasion!

Q: What looks like half a cat?
A: The other half!

Did you hear about the cat who drank 5 bowls of water? She set a new lap record!

What is the difference between a man and a cat? One eats a lot and is lazy. The other one is a pet.

Q: What side of the cat has the most fur?
A: The OUT-side!

Q: Why did the cat cross the road
A: It was the chicken's day off!

I got rid of my husband. The cat was allergic...

Q: What kind of cat will keep your grass short?
A: A Lawn Meower.

Q: What is a cat's favorite vegetable?
A: As-purr-agus!

Q: What is a kitten's favorite day of the week?
A: Caturday!

Q: Why did the cat go to Los Angeles?
A: Claws it wanted to!

Q: What do cats eat for breakfast?
A: Mice Krispies!

A wildcat meets a beaver in the forest. The beaver asks the wildcat why she smells so dreadful. The wildcat replies, "I was walking by a pooping bear and he asked me if my fur makes fuzz. I said no. So he wiped his butt with me." The beaver asks: "So how come you're still in such a good mood?" "Well," the wildcat replies, "When he was done with me, he asked the hedgehog!"

In the middle of the desert, one cat says to the other, "Oh man, I have to pee so badly." "Why don't you just go and do it?", the other cat says. "I can't. There is no litter box!"

Q: How did a cat take first prize at the bird show?
A: He just jumped up to the cage, reached in, and took it.

If Chuck Norris was a cat, he would have ten lives!

Two cats are sitting on opposite sides of a river. One cat yells to the other: "How do I get to the other side of the river?" The other cat replies: "You ARE on the other side!"

Q: Who was the most powerful cat in China?
    A: Chairman Miaow!

Don't tell me anymore funny cat jokes or I'll puma pants...

Q: What is a cat's favorite book?
A: The prince and the paw-purr!

Q: What does the lion say to his friends before they go out hunting for food?
A: "Let us prey!"

Q: Did you know that cats designed the beautiful pyramids in Egypt?
A: It was all drawn out on paw-pyrus!

Q: What do you call a cat that can handle media attention well?
A: A press kit!

One day, a cat walks in a store and asks the shop owner if he sells raspberries. The shop owner says, "No, we only sell bananas." The next day, the cat returns and asks for raspberries again. Again, the shop owner says he doesn't sell them.

When the cat returns the next day, the shop owner says: "No, you stupid cat, we don't sell raspberries! If you come back tomorrow with that same question again, I swear I will nail your paws to the floor!"

The shop owner can't believe his eyes when the cat walks into his store the very next day. This time, the cat asks, "Do you have any nails?"

The shop owner replies, "No, we don't." "Okay, good," the cat responds, "Do you sell raspberries?"

Q: What did the cat say when he lost his toys?
A: You got to be kitten me.

Q: What would a cat say if you stepped on its tail?
A: "Me-OW!"

Q: What time is it when ten cats chase a mouse?
A: Ten After One.

Q: What do cats wear when they go to bed?
A: Paw-jamas!

A teacher asks her class: "Let's say I gave you two cats, two more cats, and then another two cats; how many would you have?" Wilma answers: "Seven."

Teacher: "No, Wilma, let me repeat the question... If I gave you 2 cats, 2 more cats and then another 2, how many would you have in total?" Wilma: "7."

Teacher, getting frustrated now: "Pff, OK...Let's try this another way. If I gave you two bananas, two more bananas, and then another two, how many bananas would you have?"

Wilma: "Six."

Teacher: "Exactly! Now, if I gave you two cats, two more, and another two; how many would you have?" Wilma: "Seven!"

Teacher: "Wilma, where on earth do you get seven from?!" Wilma: "Because I already have a cat at home!"

Q: What's the difference between a cat and a comma?
A: One has claws at the end of its paws, while the other is a pause at the end of a clause!

Q: What do you call a cat that can't stop licking itself?
A: Purrr-verted!

Q: Why do cat vampires believe everything you tell them?
A: Because they're suckers!

Two criminals are about to break out of prison. The first one jumps off a wall into a trash container. The guard, alarmed by the noise, shouts "Who's there?". The criminal replies, "MEOOOW!" The guard is relieved, "Ah I see, it's just a cat." Then, the second criminal jumps, also making some noise. The guard now gets suspicious and asks, "Hello, who is there?" To which the second criminal replies, "Nobody, it's just the cat again!"

Q: Why was the cat sitting on the computer?
A: To keep an eye on the mouse!

Q: What kind of yard work do cats like the most?
A: Meowing the lawn!

Q: What type of cat has eight legs and loves to swim?
A: An octopuss!

A three-legged cat walks into a bar. He says: "I'm looking for the man who shot my paw!"

Q: What do you get if you cross a tiger with a sheep?
A: A stripey sweater!

Q: Why do cats make the best pets?
A: Because they are purr-fect!

Q: Why did the cat sleep under the car?
A: Because he wanted to wake up oily!

Q: How is a cat like a coin?
A: It has a head on one side and a tail on the other!

A man in a movie theater notices what looks like a cat sitting next to him. "Are you a cat?" asked the man, surprised. "Yes", said the cat." What are you doing at the movies?" The cat replied, "Well, I liked the book!"

Q: What happens when a dog chases a cat into a geyser?
A: It starts raining cats and dogs!

Q: Where do cats go when their tails fall off?
A: The re-tail store!

Q: What did the cat say on the phone?
A: "Can you hear meow?"

Q: Where did the kittens go for their school field trip?
A: The mewseum!

Q: What should you say to your cat when leave for school?
A: Have a mice day!

Q: What is a cat's favorite school subject?
A: HISStory!

Q: What do you get if you cross a leopard with a watchdog?
A: A terrified postman!

A man drives deep into the woods to get rid of his cat. He lets her out at an abandoned place. After 30 minutes, his wife calls him: "The cat is back…" The man growls: "Oh man…Ehm, can you put her on please? I got lost and need directions."

Q: What kind of cat eats with their ears?
A: They all do! Who removes their ears before dinner?

Q: What is a French cat's favorite pudding?
A: Chocolate mousse!

Q: Why are cats so good at video games?
A: Because they have nine lives!

Q: What is a cat's favorite color?
A: Purrrple!

Q: What did the alien say to the cat?
A: "Take me to your litter!"

Q: What is it called when a cat wins a dog show?
A: A CAT-HAS-TROPHY!

A couple were going to see a movie and ordered a taxi. As the couple left the house, their cat ran back in. The husband went back inside, because they didn't want the cat to be shut in the house while they were away. The wife stepped into the taxi. Because she didn't want the taxi driver to know that the house was empty, she told him that her husband had just gone inside to say goodbye to her mother. A short while later, her husband also stepped into the cab and said: "My apologies for taking so long, but that stupid old thing was hiding under the bed. I had to poke her with a broomstick to get her to come out!"

Q: What is the cat's favorite magazine?
A: Good Mousekeeping!

Q: How do you know cats are sensitive?
A: They cry over spilt milk!

A policeman stops a man in a car with a puma in the front seat. "What are you doing with that puma?", he asked. "You should take it to the zoo!" The next week, the same policeman sees the same man with the puma again in the front seat. This time, both are wearing sunglasses. The policeman pulls the car over. "I thought you were going to take it to the zoo!" The man replied, "I did. We had such a great time we are going to the beach this weekend!"

Q: What did the cat say to the dog?
A: Check meow-t!